RUBY

Written by Shannen Yauger

Illustrated by Bojana Stojanovic

CHAPTER 1

Ruby's Story

Imagine you are sitting in a room with a group of children. A grown-up is going to read a book to all of you.

In this room we have boys and girls with light hair and dark hair. We have boys and girls with all shades of skin.

When Ruby Bridges was a little girl, this was not possible. When she was little, she had to stay only with people that were African American.

Many people did not believe this was right, kind, or good. They did not think that people needed to be *segregated* (or kept apart) because of the color of their skin.

When Ruby was in first grade, she was one of the first African American children to go to a school that was built just for white children.

Let's follow Ruby's story as she makes history!

CHAPTER 2

Before

"Ruby! Ruby, where are you?"

Little Ruby could hear her mother yelling for her from the back door of her grandmother's house. Jumping

up from the garden, she ran toward Mama.

"Here I am, Mama!" little Ruby exclaimed. It was just starting to cool off a bit in September of 1958 in Mississippi, and four-year-old Ruby had been playing with her cousins.

"Say goodbye, child. It is
time we left for New Orleans,"
Mama said as she gently wiped
some dirt from Ruby's face.
Ruby frowned, as she was
sad to leave the farm that
her granddaddy worked on as
a sharecropper. Her cousins
all lived nearby, and she knew
she'd miss them when her
mama and papa moved her
little family one state away
to New Orleans, Louisiana.

Papa didn't want to work as a sharecropper and had a job at a service station in New Orleans. Her family would have a fresh start, her papa kept saying, but Ruby did not want to go.

"Yes, ma'am," Ruby said quietly to Mama as she went to hug her cousins and grandparents. There were no tears, since Ruby would be back to visit, but she was sad.

After a long drive, Ruby and her parents pulled up in front of a big house in the city. Ruby could hear kids yelling and cars honking their horns and lots of strange noises. It was hotter here than on the farm as well. Ruby pulled her teddy bear out of the car and slowly walked into the house.

Ruby's family rented the front part of the house, and other families lived in the back and upstairs. There was a bedroom for Papa and Mama, as well as a room for Ruby and her brothers and sister. There was a living room, too. Mama was excited about the kitchen. It had plenty of space, and Mama loved to cook.

"Ruby, help me with this stuff," Mama said as she piled bags and boxes into the kitchen. "I will make a breakfast for dinner tonight to welcome us to

our new home!" Mama smiled
her pretty smile.

"Bacon, eggs, and grits! Yum!
Could we also have banana
pudding for dessert, or sweet
potato pie?" Ruby loved Mama's
cooking, and she could tell that
the kitchen was going to be
her favorite room in their new
house.

As the weeks went on, Ruby
began to like living in the
city. Mama got a job at night

cleaning houses and hotels, and Papa worked during the day at the service station. Ruby, her brothers, and her sister grew close to one another. They loved to learn about God and listen to Papa tell them about

how God is always there to protect them. As they said their prayers with Mama each night before she went to work, they knew that God could hear them.

CHAPTER 3

The Test

Ruby was so happy to go to school. She loved to learn and worked so hard to read and to add and subtract numbers. Papa often told her how important school was, since he and Mama were unable to go.

"Work hard, little Ruby, and learn all you can," he would say each morning as she left for school. It was a long way to school at Johnson Lockett Elementary, where Ruby went to kindergarten. Johnson Lockett was a school just for African American children, and Ruby loved her school.

One morning in the spring of that year, Mama woke Ruby up early.

"Get up, little Ruby. We need to look extra nice today. You are going to take a test, and I need for you to be ready!"

Ruby was not sure what
Mama meant by a test but got
up and put on the pretty dress
Mama had set out for her. She
loved it, and it had a matching
bow and nice shoes.

"Mama, there are so many people here," Ruby whispered when they got to the testing room. Ruby looked around at the hundred or so kids in the room. All were African American, like her.

"Hush, little Ruby, and try your best," Mama said as Ruby took a seat with the other children.

Ruby picked up her pencil and started the test. It was very hard, and she wasn't sure she answered the questions the right way. They were tricky.

Many of the children did not pass that test. It was made to be very tricky.

Mama and Papa talked about

the test that night when the children went to bed.

"It was to be hard," Papa said quietly to Mama. "It was to be hard so that if our African American children don't pass, the schools can stay segregated. The white people don't want us in their schools."

Mama shook her head sadly.

"I just want Ruby to go to the best school she can," Mama said before she left for work.

Well, Ruby did do well on that test! Very few children passed the test, but Ruby did! She was chosen to go to a new school, William Frantz Public School, for first grade. Little Ruby did not know that she would make history.

CHAPTER 4

Brave Little Ruby

Ruby didn't get to start at William Frantz right away. Since some people were mad that African American children could go to their schools, they worked with the government to pass laws that would make it so that Ruby couldn't go to the white children's school. Finally a judge named Judge J.

Skelly Wright struck down all of those laws! He believed that everyone should have access to a good education, no matter the color of their skin.

On Monday, November 14, 1960,

Ruby got dressed for school, taking care to look very nice.

"Mama, why are you all dressed up?" Ruby asked. Mama just smiled.

"I want to go to your new school, too!" Mama replied. Ruby was okay with that. She felt a little scared to start at a new school.

As Ruby finished her breakfast, she heard a knock on the door. Mama jumped up and ran to answer it.

"Let's go, ma'am," Ruby heard a deep voice kindly say. Ruby put her plate in the sink, and Mama got her purse from the chair.

"Are you ready to go?" asked a second man, dressed in a nice suit. Ruby felt shy. Why were these four men at her door?

"These nice men are United States marshals, Ruby! They are here to give us a ride to school." Mama smiled her big smile. Ruby just looked up shyly and nodded her head.

Ruby and Mama got into the car with the four men, and they started the short drive to school.

When they arrived at William Frantz Public School, Ruby felt surprised. There were crowds of people at the school yelling loudly and holding signs in the air.

Little Ruby did not understand that these people were yelling awful things, were angry, and did not want her to be there.

"Mama, is it a parade?" Ruby asked.

"Hush, Ruby," Mama said, and she quickly followed the US marshal towards the school doors. Ruby tried to look at the

loud crowd of people, but the
US marshals were all around her
and she couldn't see.

Once inside the school, Ruby
and Mama went to an office
and sat down.

"Someone will see you shortly,"

a woman with short blonde hair said to Mama. "Wait here."

The woman walked off and shut another door. Ruby looked around her. This school was big and very pretty with its clean walls and floors. It must be an important place to be so clean and to have men drive you to school and people outside trying to get in!

Hour after hour, Ruby and Mama waited. People came into

the office and then left with
their children, one after another.
Ruby heard a lot of yelling, and
no one would smile at her even
if she smiled at them. Ruby was
sad. Was this a nice place? Soon
the US marshal came to see
them in the office.

"It's three o'clock, ma'am.
Let's get you home," said the
man with a small smile.

Mama stood up and looked
down at Ruby. She took Ruby's

hand, and they followed the US marshal out of the door and back into the car.

"Mama, the people are still outside of the school and yelling. Mama, I don't understand," Ruby said softly. Mama didn't answer and shook her head.

CHAPTER 5

All By Herself

When Ruby got home, she and Mama told Papa about their day.

"There were lots of people holding signs and yelling. I sat all day in the office, and lots of parents took their kids away and yelled at the principal," Ruby said as she ate her second bowl of banana pudding. Papa looked over at Mama and

shook his head. He didn't look
happy.

"You are my brave little
Ruby," he said as he kissed the
top of her head. Ruby smiled a
big, happy smile.

The next morning the US marshals came back. Mama and Ruby hopped into the car and went to the school. The people with signs were still out there, but Mama told Ruby that she should not try to read them. She and Mama prepared to sit in the office again, but instead a nice woman brought them to a classroom upstairs.

"Hi, Ruby! I am your teacher, Mrs. Henry." The lady with

blonde hair sat down in a small chair near Ruby.

"That is a very pretty dress! Did you get it just for this special day at school?" Mrs. Henry smiled at Ruby.

Ruby looked at Mama, who went to the back of the room and quietly sat down. Ruby was scared to answer Mrs. Henry. She had never been alone with a white person before, and she was scared Mrs. Henry may yell at her like the people outside had done for the past two days. Ruby felt very shy and just looked at Mrs. Henry as she nodded her head just a little bit.

"Well," said Mrs. Henry. "Let's get started! What shall we learn today?"

Ruby followed Mrs. Henry to the chalkboard and began to listen carefully to all that Mrs. Henry had to say.

The day went by quickly. Ruby didn't leave that room all day, unless she had to go to the bathroom. While it took a bit of time to get over her shyness, she decided she liked

Mrs. Henry. Each day that week, they did the same thing. They read books and played games.

For the first two days, Mama sat quietly in the back of the room. On the third day, Mama held Ruby's hands in hers when the US marshals arrived. "Today you must go to school on your own, brave little Ruby. I cannot go with you. Mrs. Henry will take care of you, and I will see you after school."

"Yes, ma'am," Ruby said with a smile. She was not scared. Mrs. Henry was so kind, and they had fun learning reading, writing, and math. The only thing Ruby wondered was where all of the other children were! Weren't there supposed to be children at a school? She could hear some, and she could smell their lunch at midday, but why didn't she ever see them?

CHAPTER 6

Other People

One morning Papa didn't leave
for work. He sat at the table
as Mama made breakfast. He
quietly said "thank you" when
Mama put his bowl of grits in
front of him. Ruby was scared.

"Papa, are you okay?" she
asked.

"I will be fine, brave little
Ruby," he answered. "Pass the

butter, please."

He smiled at Ruby and ate his grits. "Eat up, little one," he said. "You have learning to do."

While Ruby put her shoes on and waited for the marshals to arrive, she heard a man outside say that her papa had lost his job. He was fired because the station manager found out that people were angry that Ruby

went to the school for white kids. They said they would not come to his business anymore unless he fired Papa.

Ruby was sad. What had she done wrong?

Ruby went to school that day and every weekday after. She and Mrs. Henry loved their time together, so they were both there every single day.

A few weeks later, Ruby got home to find boxes of gifts in their living room.

"Mama!" she said with a big smile. "What is all of this?"

Ruby picked up a doll and a few pretty dresses and broke into a big grin.

"People heard that you were going to school and that Papa lost his job. They wanted to be kind. Isn't this all wonderful?" Mama said with her big smile. "Now pick some toys for your brothers and sister. You need to share the gifts with them, too!"

Ruby started setting aside toys that the younger children would like. Papa came home, smiling, and said a kind man hired him as a housepainter.

CHAPTER 7

Ruby's Troubles

"Mama! Papa!" yelled Ruby. She jumped out of her bed, tears running down her face.

"Ruby, what is it?" Mama asked, looking worried as Ruby ran into the room.

"I had a bad dream," Ruby said quietly. She could not remember her dream but

knew that something bad had
happened in it.

Ruby's parents looked at
one another over Ruby's head.
The bad dreams had started
a week after Ruby went to
school and had gotten worse.

"Did you say your prayers, Ruby?" Mama asked softly. "God will hear your prayers."

Ruby nodded and started to pray.

The next morning, Ruby told her Mama that she didn't want a peanut butter sandwich. She wanted to eat in the cafeteria with the other children, then play on the playground. Mama just shook her head and kept packing Ruby's lunch.

When it was time to eat, Mrs. Henry went to the teachers' room for her food. Ruby hid her sandwich in the cabinet. Maybe if she didn't have food, they would let her eat in the cafeteria. Each day Ruby hid her sandwich, until one day the man that cleaned the room told Mrs. Henry that the rats had found the sandwiches. Mrs. Henry decided to eat with Ruby so she wouldn't be alone.

"Thank you, Mrs. Henry," Ruby said with a big smile.

Bit by bit, Ruby stopped being scared and the bad dreams went away.

CHAPTER 8

Understanding

Later in the school year, when the spring flowers were starting to appear, Ruby saw other children in the school. Mrs. Henry could tell that Ruby was sad that she never got to talk to other children and went all the way to the superintendent of schools to

ask for Ruby to be able to
play with the other kids. One
day, a few kids were able to
come to Ruby and Mrs. Henry's
classroom. Ruby was so excited.
The children looked at her, and
she looked back at them.

"Would you like to play?"
Ruby asked a little boy.

He looked at the floor, the
desk, anywhere but at Ruby.
"Naw, I can't play with you,"
he said. "My mama said not to

play with you because you are
black."

Ruby's eyes got big. She did
not get mad at the boy, as he
was just obeying his mama.

All of a sudden, Ruby
understood what had happened
this past year. The people
yelling, the posters they
held, her not being able to be
around the other kids—it was
all because she was African
American and everyone else in
the school was white. Ruby did
not react with anger. She was
not mad at the boy for what
he said, but it did make her
sad.

CHAPTER 9

Later Years

The rest of first grade was a bit more fun for Ruby. The other children still came to her classroom. Ruby made a few friends. Not everyone was unkind because she was African American.

School ended, and Ruby had all summer on her grandparents' farm to run around in the sun.

When second grade started, there were no US marshals to bring Ruby to school. There were no people with posters outside of William Frantz Public School. There were even a few other African American kids at the school. But Mrs. Henry was gone.

"Mama, what should I do without Mrs. Henry?" Ruby cried. Her new teacher did not talk to her like Mrs. Henry did

and was not often kind to Ruby.
She made fun of the way Ruby
spoke and had a harsh tone
to her voice. Some of the kids
laughed at Ruby as well.

"Be my brave little Ruby,"
Papa said when Ruby talked
about school. "You can study
hard and learn from anyone,
any time." Papa always knew
how to make Ruby feel better.

Ruby went to school day
after day. She tried hard on all

of her work. She was kind to
everyone, even those who were
not kind to her. She worked

hard at school, not because she
wasn't as smart as her peers,
but because she had to work
harder. Since she was African
American, she had to prove she
had a right to be there. This
didn't make Ruby angry, though.
She chose to be strong instead.

"I am brave little Ruby," she
would say to herself if she got
scared. "God hears my prayers
and always loves me."

The Ruby Bridges Foundation

Ruby Bridges went on to finish school, graduating from an integrated high school.

After graduation, she studied travel and tourism and went on to become one of the first African Americans to work for a large travel agency in New Orleans as a travel agent. She continued this work for years, eventually marrying and having four sons. The family settled in New Orleans, the city Ruby had grown to love.

In 1999, after her brother's death, Ruby went back to William Frantz Public School to drop off her young nieces. Disturbed by what she witnessed at the inner-city school, and fueled by her desire to help all children reach their dreams, Ruby decided to take action. She became a volunteer at the school several days a week and encouraged other parents to become involved in their children's education by helping out at the school.

Thus began the Ruby Bridges Foundation, an after-school program providing cultural arts classes for young students. As the program grew, Ruby extended it to include another program called Ruby's Bridges. This program helps children understand other cultures by performing community service projects. The Ruby Bridges Foundation continues to promote understanding of all people and cultures and to create change through education and bravery.

"We all have a common enemy, and it is evil."
—Ruby Bridges

More Level 2 Books from The Good and the Beautiful Library

Princess Penny Saves the Day

By Heidi Jenkins

Helen Keller: Into the Light

By Shannen Yauger

Facts About Frogs & Snakes

By Sue Stuever Battel

Mary Helen and the Black Pony

By Molly Taylor Sanchez